DS4M TOOLKIT:
a companion for
DAILY STRENGTH FOR MEN

by Chris Bolinger

DS4M Toolkit
ISBN: 978-1724258984

A companion for:
   Daily Strength for Men: A 365-Day Devotional
   ISBN: 978-1-4245-5753-0 (faux leather)
   ISBN: 978-1-4245-5754-7 (e-book)

Using This Toolkit

This toolkit has three features that will help you get more out of the devotional, *Daily Strength for Men*: images, space, and indexes.

Images: For every two-day devotion in *Daily Strength for Men*, the toolkit provides a compelling image, which can serve as a visual reminder of the verse and the devotion. If you want to see larger, full-color versions of these images, visit the *Daily Strength for Men* website, DailyStrengthforMen.com. You have my permission to download any and all of the images.

Space: Want to jot down your notes for a verse or passage? Want to record your answers to the devotional's questions for reflection and application? There's not much room in the devotional for that. OK, there's no room for that, so I put plenty of space in the toolkit.

Indexes: These require a bit more of an explanation. I'll start by saying that I am not a fan of random.

There was nothing random about being a high-tech product manager, which was my role for most of my career. My primary responsibility was to figure out how my company could solve prospective customer problems better than competitors did. I had quantified goals, or performance objectives, with milestones and regular reviews to chart my progress. I received solid training from experts in my field. When I embarked on a project, I relied on proven tools honed by others who had done similar work before me. And I had a plan. If I executed that plan well, then I got good results and, with them, bonuses, raises, promotions, and other rewards.

My spiritual life, however, was a lot different. I had some goals there, but they were more qualitative than quantitative, and it was tough for me to tell if I was making progress. I didn't get much training. Tools were pretty scarce. And I really didn't have a plan.

I had a goal for reading my Bible. I was going to do it every day, because I knew that that would help me connect with God. But when I missed a day (or two), it was tough for me to get back in rhythm. That was especially true when I was following a reading plan, such as reading the entire Bible in a year. Once I missed a few days and got behind, I couldn't seem to catch up.

"Maybe a daily devotional is the answer," I thought. But a typical daily devotional struck me as, well, pretty random. There's a random verse for the day and the author's thoughts on that random verse. Even when the verse and the thoughts are compelling, I rarely can make use of them that day, because they are not applicable to what I'm going through. I have to file them away, for use at some later time. But my internal filing system is already overloaded.

What I wanted was a way to select each day's devotion instead of having to read what the author chose for me. I wanted the equivalent of an online search bar for the devotional.

I can't give you a search bar for *Daily Strength for Men*, so I'm giving you indexes. Lots of indexes. In addition to the table of contents, which lists the title and verse or verses for every two-day devotion, there are six indexes that you can use to decide what to read each day:

- **Topics:** Select from among 50 topics, including courage, doubting God, forgiveness, leadership, power, suffering, and work (employment). You're likely to find a topic – and a set of devotions – that is relevant to your life right now.

- **Films:** Over 20 films are discussed in devotions.

- **Songs and Hymns:** Over 30 songs, ranging from classical choral works to recent hits, are referenced in devotions.

- **Books:** from Christian classics to *Alice's Adventures in Wonderland*

- **People in the Bible:** 35 Biblical characters, from both the Old Testament and the New Testament, are discussed in devotions.

- **Other People:** some important figures from the past century

There's no right or wrong way to use *Daily Strength for Men* and this toolkit. Want to read a devotion that you've already read? Feel free. Not really interested in reading some of the devotions? You can skip them…although I'd love to hear why you did. (Contact me at DailyStrengthforMen.com, with any feedback you have on the devotional and the toolkit.)

My prayer is that *Daily Strength for Men*, and this toolkit, will get you into a rhythm of getting your daily strength from God's Word.

Table of Contents: Day-by-Day Study

Day 1	Day 2	Title	Verse(s)
Mar 28	Mar 29	A Voice from a Whirlwind	Job 42:2
Mar 30	Mar 31	With Friends Like These…	Job 42:10a
Apr 1	Apr 2	Happy and Blessed	Psalm 1:1-2
Apr 3	Apr 4	A Shield about Me	Psalm 3:3
Apr 5	Apr 6	Richest Man in Town	Psalm 6:9
Apr 7	Apr 8	Praising God in Uncertainty	Psalm 8:1
Apr 9	Apr 10	A Little Lower	Psalm 8:4-5
Apr 11	Apr 12	A Stronghold in Egypt	Psalm 9:9
Apr 13	Apr 14	A Life Navigation App	Psalm 16:11
Apr 15	Apr 16	The Apple of His Eye	Psalm 17:8
Apr 17	Apr 18	Heroic Restraint	Psalm 18:32
Apr 19	Apr 20	Nothing but Blue Skies	Psalm 19:1
Apr 21	Apr 22	Moving to a New Pasture	Psalm 23:1
Apr 23	Apr 24	Rod and Staff	Psalm 23:4
Apr 25	Apr 26	The Pursuit of Sinners	Psalm 23:6
Apr 27	Apr 28	The LORD of Hosts	Psalm 24:9-10
Apr 29	Apr 30	Fearless Stephen	Psalm 27:1a
May 1	May 2	A Gentle Reminder	Psalm 27:14
May 3	May 4	Offering Reassurance	Psalm 28:7a
May 5	May 6	A Pre-Fight Blessing	Psalm 29:11
May 7	May 8	Plenty and Famine	Psalm 31:19
May 9	May 10	Wee Little Man in Jericho	Psalm 32:5
May 11	May 12	Great and Good	Psalm 34:4
May 13	May 14	"Person to Person"	Psalm 34:5
May 15	May 16	Taste and See	Psalm 34:8
May 17	May 18	You Are Opposed	Psalm 34:19
May 19	May 20	The Desires of Your Heart	Psalm 37:4
May 21	May 22	Stand Up Eight	Psalm 37:23-24
May 23	May 24	The Patience of Joseph	Psalm 40:1-2
May 25	May 26	A Mighty Fortress	Psalm 46:1
May 27	May 28	It Is Well	Psalm 55:22
May 29	May 30	IN GOD WE TRUST	Psalm 56:3-4a
May 31	Jun 1	The Best Things in Life	Psalm 63:3
Jun 2	Jun 3	(Good) News Flash!	Psalm 68:11
Jun 4	Jun 5	Doubting Disciples	Psalm 68:18a
Jun 6	Jun 7	You Can Depend on Me	Psalm 71:3
Jun 8	Jun 9	A Rock Becomes a Failure	Psalm 73:26
Jun 10	Jun 11	A German Requiem	Psalm 84:1
Jun 12	Jun 13	Groundhog Day	Psalm 84:10a
Jun 14	Jun 15	Forgiving Every Penny	Psalm 86:5
Jun 16	Jun 17	Marvelous Things	Psalm 98:1
Jun 18	Jun 19	A Joyful Noise	Psalm 100:1
Jun 20	Jun 21	Forever	Psalm 100:5
Jun 22	Jun 23	Field of Peace	Psalm 103:2-3
Jun 24	Jun 25	Schindler's Pit	Psalm 103:4

Day 1	Day 2	Title	Verse(s)
Jun 26	Jun 27	A Spiritual Diet	Psalm 103:5
Jun 28	Jun 29	Fighting for Justice	Psalm 103:6
Jun 30	Jul 1	To Infinity, and Beyond	Psalm 103:12
Jul 2	Jul 3	Running Away Naked	Psalm 106:2
Jul 4	Jul 5	Introverts Unite!	Psalm 109:30-31
Jul 6	Jul 7	Drinking like Dogs	Psalm 118:6
Jul 8	Jul 9	Salvation on a Mountain	Psalm 118:14
Jul 10	Jul 11	Redemption in Hickory	Psalm 119:71
Jul 12	Jul 13	Sword of the Spirit	Psalm 119:105
Jul 14	Jul 15	The Bible's Knuckleheads	Psalm 119:114
Jul 16	Jul 17	Good News for the Simple	Psalm 119:130
Jul 18	Jul 19	Smelling the Color Nine	Psalm 120:1
Jul 20	Jul 21	Special Agent	Psalm 121:2
Jul 22	Jul 23	A Wonderful Life	Psalm 126:3
Jul 24	Jul 25	Steadfast and Plentiful	Psalm 130:7
Jul 26	Jul 27	Knitted Together	Psalm 139:13-14a
Jul 28	Jul 29	Lift Up Your Voice in Praise	Psalm 147:1
Jul 30	Jul 31	A City under Siege	Psalm 147:3
Aug 1	Aug 2	Bigger Than the Boogie Man	Psalm 147:5
Aug 3	Aug 4	Lord, Have Mercy	Psalm 147:6
Aug 5	Aug 6	Unbroken in Christ	Psalm 147:10-11
Aug 7	Aug 8	A Dazzling Adornment	Psalm 149:4
Aug 9	Aug 10	Risking the Den	Proverbs 1:33
Aug 11	Aug 12	The Value of Wisdom	Proverbs 2:6
Aug 13	Aug 14	Peace on the Battlefield	Proverbs 3:1-2
Aug 15	Aug 16	The Trust of Ananias	Proverbs 3:5-6
Aug 17	Aug 18	Still Standing after 15	Proverbs 3:11-12
Aug 19	Aug 20	The Wisdom of Hazel	Proverbs 3:13-14
Aug 21	Aug 22	Shading Our Eyes	Proverbs 4:18
Aug 23	Aug 24	Surprise!	Proverbs 5:21
Aug 25	Aug 26	A Straight-A Student	Proverbs 9:10
Aug 27	Aug 28	Keeping Your Hands Clean	Proverbs 11:18
Aug 29	Aug 30	A Good Neighbor	Proverbs 11:25
Aug 31	Sep 1	Rotting Bones	Proverbs 14:30
Sep 2	Sep 3	My Dog's Better	Proverbs 14:31
Sep 4	Sep 5	The First Evangelist	Proverbs 16:3
Sep 6	Sep 7	What's in a Name?	Proverbs 18:10
Sep 8	Sep 9	Sharpen His Saw	Proverbs 27:17
Sep 10	Sep 11	Turn, Turn, Turn	Ecclesiastes 3:1
Sep 12	Sep 13	Beauty at the Well	Ecclesiastes 3:11a
Sep 14	Sep 15	Songs or Tales	Ecclesiastes 4:9-10a
Sep 16	Sep 17	A Tenacious Center	Ecclesiastes 4:12
Sep 18	Sep 19	An Unspectacular Life	Ecclesiastes 12:13
Sep 20	Sep 21	The Power That Heals	Song of Solomon 8:6a
Sep 22	Sep 23	700 Years in the Making	Isaiah 7:14

Day 1	Day 2	Title	Verse(s)
Sep 24	Sep 25	Lighting the Darkness	Isaiah 9:2
Sep 26	Sep 27	At the Back of the Stage	Isaiah 9:6
Sep 28	Sep 29	Just Off Red Square	Isaiah 12:2
Sep 30	Oct 1	The Wild Man	Isaiah 25:1
Oct 2	Oct 3	The Rolling Thunder	Isaiah 25:4a
Oct 4	Oct 5	Perfect Peace for "Pistol"	Isaiah 26:3
Oct 6	Oct 7	The Rock of Ages	Isaiah 26:4
Oct 8	Oct 9	Waiting for God	Isaiah 30:18
Oct 10	Oct 11	The Crooked Straight	Isaiah 40:4
Oct 12	Oct 13	The Forgotten Part	Isaiah 40:5
Oct 14	Oct 15	Extra! Extra!	Isaiah 40:28
Oct 16	Oct 17	The Value of Strength	Isaiah 40:29
Oct 18	Oct 19	No More Weariness	Isaiah 40:30-31
Oct 20	Oct 21	A Firm Foundation	Isaiah 41:10
Oct 22	Oct 23	450 vs. 1	Isaiah 41:13
Oct 24	Oct 25	A Nu Thang	Isaiah 43:19
Oct 26	Oct 27	Overblown?	Isaiah 45:2
Oct 28	Oct 29	Like a Flint	Isaiah 50:7
Oct 30	Oct 31	Falsely Accused	Isaiah 53:3
Nov 1	Nov 2	Not a Beast	Isaiah 53:4
Nov 3	Nov 4	Amazing Love!	Isaiah 53:5
Nov 5	Nov 6	Paul the Sheep	Isaiah 53:6
Nov 7	Nov 8	No Separation	Isaiah 54:17a
Nov 9	Nov 10	Are You the One?	Isaiah 61:1
Nov 11	Nov 12	Feeling God's Pleasure	Jeremiah 1:5a
Nov 13	Nov 14	Back in Kindergarten	Jeremiah 1:7
Nov 15	Nov 16	Healing in the Dark	Jeremiah 17:14
Nov 17	Nov 18	The Good Old Days	Jeremiah 23:5
Nov 19	Nov 20	The Master Planner	Jeremiah 29:11
Nov 21	Nov 22	The One Thing	Jeremiah 33:3
Nov 23	Nov 24	The Gift of Today	Lamentations 3:22-23
Nov 25	Nov 26	Perseverance	Lamentations 3:25
Nov 27	Nov 28	Minute by Minute	Lamentations 5:19
Nov 29	Nov 30	Your True Name	Ezekiel 36:26
Dec 1	Dec 2	From a Birmingham Jail	Daniel 3:17-18
Dec 3	Dec 4	New and Improved	Daniel 7:14b
Dec 5	Dec 6	Extravagant Grace	Daniel 9:9
Dec 7	Dec 8	Fallow Ground	Hosea 10:12b
Dec 9	Dec 10	A Better Man	Joel 2:13b
Dec 11	Dec 12	Trusting and Obeying	Joel 2:32a
Dec 13	Dec 14	Good Fortune	Amos 3:7
Dec 15	Dec 16	Shameful Joy	Obadiah 12a
Dec 17	Dec 18	In the Belly	Jonah 2:1-2
Dec 19	Dec 20	Crushing Your Sins	Micah 7:19
Dec 21	Dec 22	No More Mr. Nice Guy	Nahum 1:7a

Day 1	Day 2	Title	Verse(s)
Dec 23	Dec 24	Pay-It-Forward Joy	Habakkuk 3:18
Dec 25	Dec 26	From a Distance	Zephaniah 3:17a
Dec 27	Dec 28	Your Glory Days	Haggai 2:9a
Dec 29	Dec 30	Shouting at Jesus	Zechariah 9:9
Dec 31	Jan 1	Whole Again	Malachi 4:2a

Topics

Topic(s)	Dates					
angels	Feb 4	Feb 16	Feb 18	Mar 4	Apr 5	Apr 9
	Apr 25	Apr 27	May 11	Jun 2	Jun 6	Jul 8
	Jul 22	Sep 4	Sep 24	Oct 26		
anger	Jan 17	Jan 23	Feb 16	Mar 30	Apr 17	Jun 22
	Jul 2	Aug 5	Aug 31	Dec 9	Dec 23	
army, battles, war	Jan 21	Jan 31	Feb 4	Feb 12	Feb 14	Feb 16
	Feb 24	Feb 26	Feb 28	Mar 2	Mar 14	Apr 3
	Apr 9	Apr 27	May 11	May 13	Jun 6	Jun 16
	Jul 6	Jul 12	Jul 30	Aug 5	Aug 13	Oct 22
	Oct 26	Nov 25	Dec 11	Dec 21	Dec 29	
blessings from God, including gifts and talents	Jan 7	Jan 29	Jan 31	Feb 18	Mar 26	Mar 28
	Apr 1	Apr 17	Apr 23	May 3	May 5	May 7
	May 15	May 17	May 19	May 27	May 31	Jun 4
	Jun 6	Jul 22	Aug 7	Aug 19	Aug 29	Sep 18
	Oct 8	Nov 11	Nov 23			
commandments	See Law of God.					
courage	Feb 6	Feb 12	Feb 20	Mar 22	Apr 17	May 1
	Aug 9	Sep 14	Nov 25	Dec 1		
creation (by God)	Jan 1	Jan 3	Jan 5	Jan 7	Jan 9	Apr 9
	Apr 19	May 17	Jun 16	Jul 26	Oct 2	Oct 14
devil, Satan	See evil.					
discipline	See training, discipline.					
doubting God	Jan 29	Mar 2	Mar 8	Jun 4	Jul 12	Nov 7
	Nov 9					

Topic(s)	Dates					
evil	Jan 13	Jan 19	Feb 14	Mar 10	Mar 26	Mar 28
	Apr 9	Apr 17	Apr 21	Apr 23	Apr 27	May 17
	May 19	May 25	Jul 12	Jul 24	Aug 11	Aug 13
	Sep 14	Sep 20	Oct 22	Oct 26	Nov 7	Dec 7
	Dec 11	Dec 17				
faith in God	Feb 8	Feb 14	Feb 24	Mar 4	Mar 8	Mar 26
	Apr 17	Apr 29	May 21	Jul 8	Jul 20	Sep 18
	Sep 28	Oct 4	Nov 3	Nov 5		
faithfulness of God	Feb 2	Feb 10	Mar 8	Jun 20	Sep 10	Nov 23
family	Jan 11	Jan 15	Jan 19	Jan 27	Feb 2	Feb 18
	Feb 20	Feb 26	Mar 6	Mar 14	Apr 5	Apr 11
	Apr 25	May 3	May 5	May 13	May 15	May 23
	May 27	Jun 22	Jun 28	Jul 8	Jul 14	Jul 22
	Aug 17	Aug 19	Aug 31	Sep 6	Sep 10	Sep 16
	Sep 18	Oct 30	Nov 3	Nov 11	Dec 5	
fear, anxiety, depression, distress	Jan 21	Feb 4	Feb 6	Feb 14	Feb 16	Apr 5
	Apr 11	Apr 29	May 3	May 7	May 11	May 29
	Jul 6	Sep 10	Sep 30	Oct 4	Oct 10	Oct 18
	Oct 20	Oct 22	Nov 3	Nov 21	Dec 9	Dec 17
fear of (respect for) God	Jan 11	Mar 26	Mar 28	May 3	May 7	Aug 5
	Aug 25	Sep 18	Dec 31			
friendships	Jan 27	Feb 14	Feb 20	Feb 24	Feb 26	Mar 28
	Mar 30	Apr 5	Jun 14	Jun 28	Jul 22	Aug 19
	Aug 29	Sep 14	Sep 16	Nov 1	Dec 15	
forgiveness	Mar 2	Mar 10	Apr 13	Apr 27	May 9	May 11
	May 13	Jun 14	Jun 20	Jun 22	Jun 30	Jul 24
	Aug 31	Sep 20	Oct 6	Dec 5	Dec 7	Dec 19
foundation	Feb 10	Oct 20	Oct 28			
gifts from God	*See blessings from God.*					
glory of God	Feb 8	Apr 3	Apr 9	Apr 19	Apr 27	Sep 24
	Oct 2	Oct 10	Oct 12	Nov 7		
goodness of God	Jan 3	Jan 7	Jan 19	Mar 8	Mar 30	Apr 1
	Apr 21	Apr 23	Apr 25	May 7	May 11	May 15
	Jun 14	Jun 20	Nov 7	Nov 25	Dec 21	

Topic(s)	Dates					
grace of God	Jan 29	Apr 23	May 11	Jun 28	Jul 24	Aug 21
	Oct 6	Oct 8	Nov 5	Dec 5	Dec 7	Dec 9
	Dec 15					
greatness of God	Mar 28	Mar 30	Apr 7	Apr 19	Apr 27	May 11
	May 25	Jun 10	Jul 22	Aug 1	Sep 24	Oct 2
	Oct 10	Oct 12	Oct 14	Nov 23	Dec 21	
grief, mourning	Feb 4	Mar 28	May 7	May 27	Jun 10	Aug 23
	Oct 30	Nov 1	Nov 9			
guidance of God	Feb 8	Mar 2	Apr 21	Apr 23	Jun 26	Jul 16
	Jul 18	Sep 4	Oct 8	Dec 17	Dec 27	
happiness	*See joy.*					
healing	Jan 25	Mar 6	Mar 10	Jun 22	Jul 30	Sep 20
	Oct 18	Nov 3	Nov 9	Nov 15	Dec 25	Dec 31
heaven	Jan 3	Mar 10	Apr 5	Apr 9	Apr 13	Apr 25
	May 11	Jun 4	Jun 10	Nov 9	Dec 31	
hope	Jul 14	Jul 24	Aug 5	Aug 7	Oct 18	Nov 19
	Dec 13	Dec 29				
husband	*See marriage (love relationships).*					
joy	Mar 20	Apr 1	Apr 13	May 9	May 31	Jun 2
	Jun 10	Jun 18	Jul 22	Jul 30	Nov 15	Dec 11
	Dev 15	Dec 23	Dec 29			
knowledge	*See wisdom.*					
Law of God (commandments)	Jan 23	Jan 25	Jan 31	Mar 2	Mar 16	Mar 20
	Apr 1	May 19	May 29	Jul 24	Aug 11	Aug 13
	Aug 29	Sep 18	Oct 26	Nov 1	Nov 5	Nov 29
leadership	Jan 21	Feb 6	Feb 8	Feb 12	Feb 14	Feb 16
	Feb 24	Apr 11	Jul 6	Aug 1	Aug 9	Aug 19
	Aug 25	Sep 8	Nov 19	Dec 1	Dec 29	
light	Jan 3	Apr 19	Apr 29	Jul 12	Jul 16	Aug 21
	Sep 24	Oct 18	Nov 7	Dec 11		
love of God	Jan 1	Jan 29	Feb 2	Feb 26	Mar 8	Mar 12
	Apr 19	May 11	May 31	Jun 14	Jun 16	Jun 20
	Jun 24	Jul 24	Aug 5	Aug 7	Aug 17	Sep 12
	Sep 20	Sep 30	Nov 3	Nov 23	Dec 7	Dec 9

Topic(s)	Dates					
marriage (love relationships)	Jan 9	Jan 11	Jan 15	Feb 20	Mar 20	Mar 22
	May 3	May 13	Jun 12	Aug 5	Aug 23	Sep 10
	Sep 16	Sep 20	Dec 7	Dec 9		
obedience	Feb 28	Mar 16	Jun 18	Jul 8	Aug 9	Aug 15
	Sep 18	Oct 26	Nov 17	Dec 1	Dec 11	Dec 17
patience, waiting	Feb 16	May 1	May 7	May 23	Jul 18	Oct 8
	Oct 18	Nov 23	Nov 25			
peace of God	Jan 29	Apr 27	May 5	May 27	Jun 22	Jul 28
	Aug 13	Aug 31	Sep 26	Oct 4	Nov 3	Dec 29
plans of God	Jan 17	Feb 6	Feb 28	Mar 2	Mar 22	Apr 11
	Apr 29	May 23	Jul 6	Jul 8	Sep 4	Sep 30
	Oct 8	Nov 19				
power	Jan 25	Jan 31	Feb 8	Feb 18	Mar 4	Mar 16
	Mar 28	Apr 7	Apr 9	Apr 11	Apr 27	May 11
	May 15	May 17	May 25	Jun 4	Jul 12	Aug 1
	Sep 6	Sep 10	Sep 20	Oct 14	Oct 16	Oct 18
	Oct 26	Dec 25				
praying, prayers	Jan 29	Feb 4	Mar 10	Mar 30	Apr 5	May 3
	May 11	Jun 6	Jun 18	Jul 18	Jul 30	Aug 3
	Aug 9	Aug 11	Aug 31	Sep 10	Sep 18	Sep 26
	Sep 28	Nov 15	Nov 19	Nov 23	Nov 25	Dec 17
	Dec 21					
promises of God	Jan 13	Jan 15	Jan 21	Feb 8	Feb 12	Mar 2
	Apr 11	Jul 8	Aug 11	Aug 27	Oct 20	Nov 17
	Nov 21	Nov 29	Dec 27	Dec 29		
protection provided by God	Jan 9	Jan 13	Feb 10	Feb 28	Mar 2	Mar 26
	Apr 3	Apr 11	Apr 21	Apr 23	May 15	May 25
	Jun 6	Jul 20	Aug 9	Sep 6	Oct 20	Oct 26
refuge	*See protection provided by God.*					
repentance	Jan 23	Mar 10	Mar 28	Mar 30	Apr 9	Apr 25
	May 11	Jun 14	Jun 30	Aug 31	Dec 5	Dec 17
restoration	Feb 26	Mar 30	May 9	May 23	Aug 31	Dec 5
sacrifice	Jan 25	Feb 26	Apr 11	Jul 8	Jul 20	Aug 11
	Sep 14	Sep 18	Oct 22	Nov 3		
safety	*See protection provided by God.*					

Topic(s)	Dates					
salvation: God offers salvation through Jesus	Jan 21	Feb 10	Feb 28	Apr 13	Apr 29	May 9
	May 11	Jun 16	Jul 4	Jul 8	Jul 20	Aug 5
	Aug 7	Sep 2	Sep 28	Oct 6	Oct 26	Oct 30
	Nov 3	Nov 9	Nov 27	Dec 11	Dec 23	Dec 29
	Dec 31					
sheep, shepherd	Feb 6	Apr 9	Apr 21	Apr 23	Apr 25	Jun 20
	Jul 16	Jul 24	Sep 24	Oct 28	Nov 5	Nov 17
strength	Jan 9	Jan 21	Feb 6	Feb 10	Feb 12	Feb 14
	Feb 18	Feb 22	Feb 24	Feb 28	Mar 12	Mar 18
	Mar 20	Mar 22	Apr 17	Apr 27	May 1	May 3
	May 5	May 7	May 25	Jun 6	Jun 8	Jul 8
	Jul 12	Aug 1	Aug 5	Aug 19	Aug 29	Sep 6
	Sep 14	Sep 16	Sep 20	Sep 28	Oct 2	Oct 16
	Oct 18	Oct 20	Nov 1	Nov 13	Dec 1	Dec 21
suffering	Mar 8	Mar 26	Mar 28	Mar 30	May 21	Jul 10
	Jul 28	Jul 30	Aug 5	Aug 7	Oct 30	Nov 1
	Dec 15					
training, discipline	Jan 7	Feb 12	Mar 18	Apr 1	May 5	Jul 20
	Aug 5	Aug 13	Aug 17	Aug 21	Aug 25	Sep 8
	Nov 11					
trusting God	Jan 15	Feb 6	Feb 20	Mar 2	Mar 22	Apr 21
	May 3	May 7	May 13	May 17	May 23	May 29
	Jun 20	Jul 8	Jul 18	Jul 20	Aug 15	Sep 28
	Oct 4	Oct 6	Nov 13	Dec 11		
war	*See army, battles, war.*					
wife	*See marriage (love relationships).*					
wisdom	Feb 10	Jul 18	Jul 20	Aug 11	Aug 19	Aug 25
	Sep 10	Nov 13				
Word of God	Mar 2	Mar 10	May 29	Jun 12	Jun 26	Jul 12
	Jul 14	Jul 16	Jul 18	Aug 13	Aug 25	Dec 13
work (employment)	Jan 7	Jan 27	Mar 18	Mar 20	Apr 5	Apr 7
	May 13	May 27	Jun 6	Jun 24	Jun 28	Jul 22
	Aug 1	Aug 27	Sep 4	Sep 10	Oct 4	Nov 5
	Nov 19					
worship	Jan 23	Jan 29	Mar 4	Mar 26	Apr 9	May 25
	Jun 4	Jun 10	Jun 12	Jun 18	Aug 9	Sep 10
	Sep 24	Oct 14	Oct 18	Oct 22	Dec 1	

References to Films, Songs, Books, and People

Films

Film	Date(s)
As Good As It Gets	Dec 9
The Breakfast Club	Feb 24
Captain America: The First Avenger	Oct 16
Chariots of Fire	Nov 11
City Slickers	Nov 21
Field of Dreams	Mar 6 Jun 22
The Firm	Aug 27
Forrest Gump	Jul 16 Nov 23
Groundhog Day	Jun 12
Hoosiers	Jul 10
It's a Wonderful Life	Apr 5 Jul 22
Jonah: A VeggieTales Movie	Dec 17
The Lord of the Rings: The Two Towers	Sep 14
The Lord of the Rings: The Return of the King	Nov 1
Rocky	Aug 17
Rocky II	May 5
Rudy	Mar 14
The Song	Sep 10 Sep 20
Spider-Man	Feb 18
Unbroken	Aug 5
The Usual Suspects	Nov 7

Songs and Hymns

Song, Songwriter or Performer	Date
"All Creatures of Our God and King"	Jul 28
"All People that on Earth Do Dwell"	Jun 20
"And Can It Be (Amazing Love)"	Nov 3
"Beast of Burden", The Rolling Stones	Nov 1
"Benediction", Susan Ashton	Jan 29
"The Best Things in Life Are Free"	May 31
"Come Thou Font of Every Blessing"	Apr 23
"From a Distance", Bette Midler	Dec 25
A German Requiem, Brahms	Jun 10
"Glory Days", Bruce Springsteen	Dec 27
Messiah, Handel:	
"Comfort Ye" / "Ev'ry Valley"	Oct 10
"And the Glory of the Lord"	Oct 12
"For Unto Us a Child Is Born"	Sep 26

Song, Songwriter or Performer	Date
"Lift Up Your Heads"	Apr 27
"I Know That My Redeemer Liveth"	Mar 26
"How Firm a Foundation"	Oct 20
"How Great Thou Art"	Oct 2
"How Majestic Is Your Name", Michael W. Smith	Apr 7
"In the Belly of the Whale", Newsboys	Dec 17
"Is the Brightness Still in Me?", Charlie Peacock	Aug 21
"It Is Well with My Soul"	May 27
"It's Still Rock and Roll to Me", Billy Joel	Aug 25
"The Joy of the Lord", Twila Paris	Mar 20
"Keeping the Faith", Billy Joel	Nov 17
"Kyrie", Mr. Mister	Aug 3
"Lay Your Hands on Me", Thompson Twins	Jan 25
"Life Means So Much", Chris Rice	Nov 23
"A Mighty Fortress Is Our God"	May 25
"Missing Love", PFR	Dec 31
"Now Thank We All Our God"	Jul 30
"Nu Thang", dcTalk	Oct 24
"Ocean Floor", Audio Adrenaline	Dec 19
"Rock of Ages"	Oct 6
"Seasons of Love"	Nov 27
"Smell the Color 9", Chris Rice	Jul 18
"The Song (Awaken Love)"	Sep 20
"Step by Step", Rich Mullins	Sep 30
"Trust and Obey"	Dec 11

Books

Author	Title	Date(s)
Richard Adams	Watership Down	Aug 19
Lewis Carroll	Alice's Adventures in Wonderland	Apr 13
Paul Coughlin	No More Christian Nice Guy	Dec 21
John Eldredge	The Journey of Desire	Aug 7
John Eldredge	Waking the Dead	Apr 27 May 17 Oct 26
John Eldredge	Wild at Heart	Nov 29
Robert Fulghum	All I Really Need to Know I Learned in Kindergarten	Nov 13
C.S. Lewis	Mere Christianity	Mar 10 May 17
C.S. Lewis	The Lion, The Witch & The Wardrobe	Dec 21
Richards/Gonzales	The Privileged Planet	Jan 1
Dick Staub	About You: Fully Human, Fully Alive	Jan 5
Lee Strobel	The Case for Faith	Mar 8

People in the Bible

Person	Date(s)						
Abraham	Jan 15	Jan 17	Jan 21	Feb 2	Jul 8	Jul 14	Sep 6
	Nov 5	Nov 29					
Adam	Jan 7	Jan 9	Jan 27	Feb 2	Nov 7		
Ananias	Aug 15						
Barak/Deborah	Feb 14						
Daniel	Feb 4	Apr 9	Jun 16	Aug 9	Dec 1	Dec 3	Dec 5
David	Jan 31	Feb 26	Feb 28	Mar 2	Mar 8	Apr 1	Apr 3
	Apr 13	Apr 21	Apr 23	May 1	May 7	May 11	May 15
	May 17	May 19	May 21	May 25	May 29	May 31	Jun 2
	Jun 6	Jun 8	Jun 16	Jun 20	Jun 30	Jul 14	Jul 16
	Jul 20	Aug 11	Sep 26	Nov 17	Dec 5		
Elijah	Mar 4	Oct 22					
Esther	Mar 22						
Ezra	Mar 16						
Eve	Jan 7	Jan 9	Jan 27	Nov 7			
Gideon	Feb 16	Jul 6					
Hannah/Eli	May 3						
Isaac	Jan 15	Jan 21	Jul 8	Sep 6			
Jacob (Israel)	Jan 19	Jan 21	Jan 29	Feb 2	Apr 11	Apr 15	Jul 8
	Sep 6	Sep 12	Nov 29				
Jesus	Jan 3	Jan 5	Jan 23	Jan 25	Feb 2	Feb 10	Mar 20
	Mar 26	Apr 1	Apr 9	Apr 13	Apr 17	Apr 23	Apr 25
	Apr 29	May 9	May 11	May 15	May 19	Jun 2	Jun 4
	Jun 8	Jun 14	Jun 16	Jun 18	Jun 30	Jul 2	Jul 8
	Jul 14	Jul 16	Jul 18	Jul 24	Aug 3	Aug 5	Aug 11
	Aug 13	Aug 15	Aug 25	Aug 29	Aug 31	Sep 4	Sep 12
	Sep 14	Sep 22	Sep 24	Sep 28	Oct 4	Oct 10	Oct 18
	Oct 26	Oct 28	Oct 30	Nov 1	Nov 3	Nov 5	Nov 7
	Nov 9	Nov 17	Nov 25	Nov 27	Dec 3	Dec 5	Dec 7
	Dec 13	Dev 15	Dec 21	Dec 25	Dec 29	Dec 31	
Job	Mar 24	Mar 26	Mar 28	Mar 30	May 23	Dec 21	
John (disciple)	Jun 2	Jul 14	Sep 4	Dec 25			
John (Baptist)	Nov 9						
Jonah	Dec 17						

Person	Date(s)						
Jonathan	Feb 26						
Joseph	Jan 19	Jan 21	May 7	May 23			
Joshua	Feb 8	Feb 12	Feb 14	Jun 16			
Mark	Jul 2						
Moses	Jan 21	Jan 23	Feb 6	Feb 8	Feb 12	Mar 2	Mar 16
	Mar 26	Apr 11	Apr 29	Sep 6			
Noah	Jan 13	May 11					
Paul	Apr 29	May 19	Jul 2	Jul 14	Aug 15	Nov 5	Dec 11
Peter	Feb 10	Jun 2	Jun 8	Jun 14	Jul 2	Jul 14	Sep 4
	Dec 11	Dec 25					
Philip	Sep 4						
Ruth	Feb 20						
Samson	Feb 18						
Sarah	Jan 15	May 3	Jul 8	Jul 14			
Solomon	Jun 6	Jul 14	Aug 11	Aug 25	Sep 2	Sep 10	Sep 16
	Sep 18	Sep 20	Oct 22	Nov 17	Dec 5		
Stephen	Apr 29	Aug 15					
Zacchaeus	May 9						

Other People

Person	Date
Lance Armstrong	Feb 22
Agatha Christie	Aug 23
Winston Churchill	Nov 25
Martin Luther	May 25
Martin Luther King, Jr.	Dec 1
Eric Liddell	Nov 11
Pete Maravich	Oct 4
Michael Phelps	Mar 18
Jackie Robinson	Apr 17
Oskar Schindler	Jun 24
Phil Vischer	Aug 1
John Wayne	Jun 6
William Wilberforce	Jun 28
Louis Zamperini	Aug 5

Jan 1

Jan 2

Created for You

In the beginning,
God created the heavens
and the earth.
– Genesis 1:1

Your notes on **Genesis 1:1-2, 26-28** and **Isaiah 45:18-19**:

Your answers to the devotional questions on January 2:

Your prayers:

Jan 3

Jan 4

Let There Be Light

And God said,
"Let there be light,"
and there was light.
– *Genesis 1:3*

Your notes on **Genesis 1:3-5** and **John 1:1-10**:

Your answers to the devotional questions on January 4:

Your prayers:

Jan 5

Jan 6

The Image of God

So God created man in his own image, in the image of God he created him; male and female he created them.
– *Genesis 1:27*

Your notes on **Genesis 1:24-28, 31**:

Your answers to the devotional questions on January 6:

Your prayers:

Jan 7

Jan 8

Working to Thrive

And God saw everything that he had made, and behold, it was very good. And there was evening and there was morning, the sixth day.
– *Genesis 1:31*

Your notes on **Genesis 1:28-31** and **Genesis 2:15-17**:

Your answers to the devotional questions on January 8:

Your prayers:

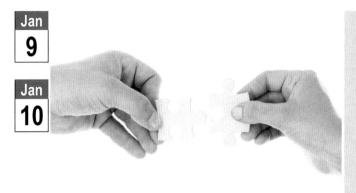

Jan 9

Jan 10

A Perfect Match

Then the Lord God said,
"It is not good that the man
should be alone; I will make
him a helper fit for him."
– Genesis 2:18

Your notes on **Genesis 2:18-23**:

Your answers to the devotional questions on January 10:

Your prayers:

Jan 11

Jan 12

Cleaving

Therefore a man shall leave his father and his mother and hold fast to his wife, and they shall become one flesh.
– Genesis 2:24

Your notes on **Genesis 2:21-25** and **Matthew 19:3-8**:

Your answers to the devotional questions on January 12:

Your prayers:

Jan 13

Jan 14

The Promise of the Rainbow

When I bring clouds over the earth and the bow is seen in the clouds, I will remember my covenant that is between me and you and every living creature of all flesh. And the waters shall never again become a flood to destroy all flesh.
– Genesis 9:14-15

Your notes on **Genesis 9:1, 8-16**:

Your answers to the devotional questions on January 14:

Your prayers:

Jan 15

Jan 16

Promising the Impossible

And he brought him outside and said, "Look toward heaven, and number the stars, if you are able to number them." Then he said to him, "So shall your offspring be." And he believed the Lord, and he counted it to him as righteousness.
— *Genesis 15:5-6*

Your notes on **Genesis 15:1-6** and **Romans 4:18, 20-25**:

Your answers to the devotional questions on January 16:

Your prayers:

Haggling with God

Then he said, "Oh let not the Lord be angry, and I will speak again but this once. Suppose ten are found there." He answered, "For the sake of ten I will not destroy it."
– *Genesis 18:32*

Your notes on **Genesis 18:23-26, 28-32**:

Your answers to the devotional questions on January 18:

Your prayers:

Redeeming an Evil Act

"As for you, you meant evil against me, but God meant it for good, to bring it about that many people should be kept alive, as they are today."
– *Genesis 50:20*

Your notes on **Genesis 49:1-2, 26; 50:15-21**:

Your answers to the devotional questions on January 20:

Your prayers:

Jan 21

Jan 22

God Comes Through

The LORD is my strength and my song, and he has become my salvation.
– Exodus 15:2a

Your notes on **Exodus 14:26-29; 15:1-2, 4-7a**:

Your answers to the devotional questions on January 22:

Your prayers:

Jan 23

Jan 24

Smashing Tablets

The Lord said to Moses, "Cut for yourself two tablets of stone like the first, and I will write on the tablets the words that were on the first tablets, which you broke."
— *Exodus 34:1*

Your notes on **Exodus 32:15-20; 34:1, 6-7**:

Your answers to the devotional questions on January 24:

Your prayers:

Magic in Your Touch

He shall lay his hand on the head of the burnt offering, and it shall be accepted for him to make atonement for him.
– Leviticus 1:4

Your notes on **Leviticus 1:1-9** and **Hosea 6:6**:

Your answers to the devotional questions on January 26:

Your prayers:

Sibling Rivalry

"You shall not take vengeance or bear a grudge against the sons of your own people, but you shall love your neighbor as yourself: I am the Lord."
– Leviticus 19:18

Your notes on **Leviticus 19:13-18** and **Hebrews 11:4**:

Your answers to the devotional questions on January 28:

Your prayers:

Jan 29

Jan 30

Demanding a Benediction

The Lord bless you and keep you; the Lord make his face to shine upon you and be gracious to you; the Lord lift up his countenance upon you and give you peace.
– *Numbers 6:24-26*

Your notes on **Numbers 6:22-27**, **Hebrews 13:20-21**, and **Jude 24-25**:

Your answers to the devotional questions on January 30:

Your prayers:

Jan 31

Feb 1

Our Mighty Resources

"Hear, O Israel: The Lord our God, the Lord is one. You shall love the Lord your God with all your heart and with all your soul and with all your might."
– *Deuteronomy 6:4-5*

Your notes on **Deuteronomy 6:1-2, 4-6** and **Mark 12:28-31**:

Your answers to the devotional questions on February 1:

Your prayers:

Feb 2

Feb 3

Who's Your Daddy?

But it is because the LORD loves you and is keeping the oath that he swore to your fathers, that the LORD has brought you out with a mighty hand and redeemed you.
 — *Deuteronomy 7:8a*

Your notes on **Deuteronomy 7:6-14a**:

Your answers to the devotional questions on February 3:

Your prayers:

Feb 4

Feb 5

God's "Silence"

"… for the LORD your God is he who goes with you to fight for you against your enemies, to give you the victory."
— *Deuteronomy 20:4*

Your notes on **Deuteronomy 20:1-4** and **Daniel 10:10-14**:

Your answers to the devotional questions on February 5:

Your prayers:

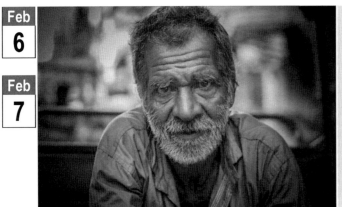

Feb 6

Feb 7

Courage Begins at 80

"Be strong and courageous.
Do not fear or be in dread
of them, for it is the LORD
your God who goes with you.
He will not leave you
or forsake you."
– *Deuteronomy 31:6*

Your notes on **Deuteronomy 31:1-3, 6** and **Exodus 4:10-15**:

Your answers to the devotional questions on February 7:

Your prayers:

Four Promises

"It is the LORD who goes before you. He will be with you; he will not leave you or forsake you. Do not fear or be dismayed."
— *Deuteronomy 31:8*

Your notes on **Deuteronomy 31:7-8** and **Joshua 1:1-5**:

Your answers to the devotional questions on February 9:

Your prayers:

Feb 10

Feb 11

The Rock

"The Rock, his work is perfect, for all his ways are justice. A God of faithfulness and without iniquity, just and upright is he."
– *Deuteronomy 32:4*

Your notes on **Deuteronomy 32:1, 3-4** and **Matthew 16:13-19**:

Your answers to the devotional questions on February 11:

Your prayers:

A Pregame Pep Talk

"Have I not commanded you? Be strong and courageous. Do not be frightened, and do not be dismayed, for the LORD your God is with you wherever you go."
— Joshua 1:9

Your notes on **Joshua 1:5-11, 16-17a**:

Your answers to the devotional questions on February 13:

Your prayers:

Fear of Leading

"That the leaders took the lead in Israel, that the people offered themselves willingly, bless the LORD!"
— *Judges 5:2*

Your notes on **Judges 4:12-16, 5:1-5**:

Your answers to the devotional questions on February 15:

Your prayers:

Testing God's Patience

Then Gideon said to God, "Let not your anger burn against me; let me speak just once more. Please let me test just once more with the fleece. Please let it be dry on the fleece only, and on all the ground let there be dew." And God did so that night; and it was dry on the fleece only, and on all the ground there was dew.
— *Judges 6:39-40*

Your notes on **Judges 6:12-15, 36-40**:

Your answers to the devotional questions on February 17:

Your prayers:

Feb 18

Feb 19

With Great Power...

But the hair of his head
began to grow again
after it had been shaved.
— *Judges 16:22*

Your notes on **Judges 16:18-22, 28-30**:

Your answers to the devotional questions on February 19:

Your prayers:

Feb 20

Feb 21

Leaving Home

But Ruth said, "Do not urge me to leave you or to return from following you. For where you go I will go, and where you lodge I will lodge. Your people shall be my people, and your God my God."
– *Ruth 1:16*

Your notes on **Ruth 1:11-19a, 22**:

Your answers to the devotional questions on February 21:

Your prayers:

Lance's Rise and Fall

The LORD makes poor
and makes rich; he brings low
and he exalts.
— 1 Samuel 2:7

Your notes on **1 Samuel 1:10-11, 2:1-7**:

Your answers to the devotional questions on February 23:

Your prayers:

Feb 24

Feb 25

An Essay for Mr. Vernon

"For the LORD sees not as man sees: man looks on the outward appearance, but the LORD looks on the heart."
– *1 Samuel 16:7b*

Your notes on **1 Samuel 16:4-13a**:

Your answers to the devotional questions on February 25:

Your prayers:

Feb 26

Feb 27

Sacrificial Love

And David said to him, "Do not fear, for I will show you kindness for the sake of your father Jonathan, and I will restore to you all the land of Saul your father, and you shall eat at my table always."
– 2 Samuel 9:7

Your notes on **2 Samuel 9:1-10**:

Your answers to the devotional questions on February 27:

Your prayers:

A Part of the Plan

"The LORD is my rock and my fortress and my deliverer, my God, my rock, in whom I take refuge, my shield, and the horn of my salvation, my stronghold and my refuge, my savior."
– *2 Samuel 22:2b-3a*

Your notes on **2 Samuel 22:1-7, 17-20**:

Your answers to the devotional questions on March 1:

Your prayers:

Mar 2

Mar 3

Your notes on **2 Samuel 22:26-33, 47-51**:

Your answers to the devotional questions on March 3:

Your prayers:

Mar 4

Mar 5

Not a Perfect Prophet

The LORD listened to the voice of Elijah. And the life of the child came into him again, and he revived.
– *1 Kings 17:22*

Your notes on **1 Kings 17:17–22** and **1 Kings 19:1–4**:

Your answers to the devotional questions on March 5:

Your prayers:

Mar 6

Mar 7

Having a Catch

Then he went to the spring of water and threw salt in it and said, "Thus says the LORD, I have healed this water; from now on neither death nor miscarriage shall come from it."
– *2 Kings 2:21*

Your notes on **2 Kings 2:19–22, Matthew 5:13,** and **Colossians 4:2-6**:

Your answers to the devotional questions on March 7:

Your prayers:

Mar 8

Mar 9

God Is Good

Oh give thanks to the
LORD, for he is good; for
his steadfast love
endures forever!
– *1 Chronicles 16:34*

Your notes on **1 Chronicles 16:7, 28–34** and **Psalm 13:1–6**:

Your answers to the devotional questions on March 9:

Your prayers:

Mar 10

Mar 11

Step by Step

"If my people who are called by my name humble themselves, and pray and seek my face and turn from their wicked ways, then I will hear from heaven and will forgive their sin and heal their land."
– 2 Chronicles 7:14

Your notes on **2 Chronicles 7:11b–20**:

Your answers to the devotional questions on March 11:

Your prayers:

Mar 12

Mar 13

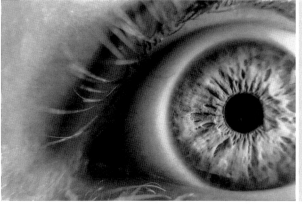

When You're Awake

For the eyes of the LORD
range throughout the earth
to strengthen those whose
hearts are fully committed
to him.
– *2 Chronicles 16:9a (NIV)*

Your notes on **2 Chronicles 16:7-9** and **Psalm 34:11-19**:

Your answers to the devotional questions on March 13:

Your prayers:

Your notes on **2 Chronicles 20:1-4, 14-17**:

Your answers to the devotional questions on March 15:

Your prayers:

Commanding Respect

And the king granted him all
that he asked, for the hand of
the LORD his God was on him.
– *Ezra 7:6b*

Your notes on **Ezra 7:6, 10-13, 25-28a**:

Your answers to the devotional questions on March 17:

Your prayers:

Mar 18

Mar 19

Training to Win

And they said, "Let us rise up and build." So they strengthened their hands for the good work.
– *Nehemiah 2:18b*

Your notes on **Nehemiah 2:13-15, 17-18** and **1 Corinthians 9:24-27**:

Your answers to the devotional questions on March 19:

Your prayers:

Mar 20

Mar 21

Unlocking Joy

"…the joy of the LORD is your strength."
— *Nehemiah 8:10b*

Your notes on **Nehemiah 8:9-12** and **James 1:2-4, 12-13, 17**:

Your answers to the devotional questions on March 21:

Your prayers:

Mar 22

Mar 23

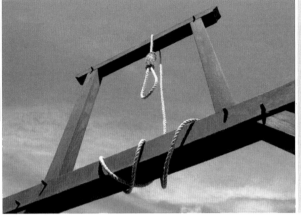

Esther's Courage

And who knows whether
you have not come to
the kingdom for such
a time as this?
— *Esther 4:14b*

Your notes on **Esther 4:9-17**:

Your answers to the devotional questions on March 23:

Your prayers:

Mar 24

Mar 25

Two Imposters

And he said, "Naked I came from my mother's womb, and naked shall I return. The LORD gave, and the LORD has taken away; blessed be the name of the LORD."
– *Job 1:21*

Your notes on **Job 1:13-22**:

Your answers to the devotional questions on March 25:

Your prayers:

Mar 26

Mar 27

A Soprano's Sweet Song

For I know that my Redeemer lives, and at the last he will stand upon the earth. And after my skin has been thus destroyed, yet in my flesh I shall see God.
— Job 19:25-26

Your notes on **Job 19:23-27** and **1 Corinthians 15:12–22**:

Your answers to the devotional questions on March 27:

Your prayers:

Mar 28

Mar 29

A Voice from a Whirlwind

I know that you can do all
things, and that no purpose
of yours can be thwarted.
— *Job 42:2*

Your notes on **Job 38:1-9, 42:1-6**:

Your answers to the devotional questions on March 28:

Your prayers:

With Friends Like These…

And the LORD restored the
fortunes of Job, when he
had prayed for his friends.
– Job 42:10a

Your notes on **Job 42:7-13, 16-17**:

Your answers to the devotional questions on March 30:

Your prayers:

Apr 1

Apr 2

Happy and Blessed

Blessed is the man who walks not in the counsel of the wicked, nor stands in the way of sinners, nor sits in the seat of scoffers; but his delight is in the law of the LORD, and on his law he meditates day and night.
– *Psalm 1:1-2*

Your notes on **Psalm 1:1-6** and **Psalm 119:1-8**:

Your answers to the devotional questions on April 2:

Your prayers:

| Apr 3 | |
| Apr 4 | |

A Shield About Me

But you, O LORD, are a shield about me, my glory, and the lifter of my head.
– *Psalm 3:3*

Your notes on **Psalm 3:1-8** and **Ephesians 6:13-18a**:

Your answers to the devotional questions on April 4:

Your prayers:

Apr 5

Apr 6

Richest Man in Town

The LORD has heard my plea; the LORD accepts my prayer.
– Psalm 6:9

Your notes on **Psalm 6:1-10** and **1 Thessalonians 5:16-19**:

Your answers to the devotional questions on April 6:

Your prayers:

Apr 7

Apr 8

Praising God in Uncertainty

O LORD, our LORD, how majestic is your name in all the earth! You have set your glory above the heavens.
-- *Psalm 8:1*

Your notes on **Psalm 8:1-3, 9** and **2 Peter 1:16-21**:

Your answers to the devotional questions on April 8:

Your prayers:

A Little Lower

What is man that you are mindful of him, and the son of man that you care for him? Yet you have made him a little lower than the heavenly beings and crowned him with glory and honor.
– *Psalm 8:4-5*

Your notes on **Psalm 8:3-8** and **Hebrews 1:1-6**:

Your answers to the devotional questions on April 10:

Your prayers:

A Stronghold in Egypt

The LORD is a stronghold for the oppressed, a stronghold in times of trouble.
— *Psalm 9:9*

Your notes on **Psalm 9:7-14** and **Exodus 15:1-3**:

Your answers to the devotional questions on April 12:

Your prayers:

A Life Navigation App

You make known to me
the path of life; in your
presence there is fullness
of joy; at your right hand are
pleasures forevermore.
– Psalm 16:11

Your notes on **Psalm 16:1-11**:

Your answers to the devotional questions on April 14:

Your prayers:

The Apple of His Eye

Keep me as the apple of
your eye; hide me in the
shadow of your wings.
– *Psalm 17:8*

Your notes on **Psalm 18:1-6, 25-32**:

Your answers to the devotional questions on April 16:

Your prayers:

Apr 17

Apr 18

Heroic Restraint

It is God who arms me
with strength and keeps
my way secure.
– *Psalm 18:32 (NIV)*

Your notes on **Psalm 18:1-6, 25-32**:

Your answers to the devotional questions on April 18:

Your prayers:

Apr 19

Apr 20

Nothing but Blue Skies

The heavens declare
the glory of God, and
the sky above proclaims
his handiwork.
— *Psalm 19:1*

Your notes on **Psalm 19:1-14**:

Your answers to the devotional questions on April 20:

Your prayers:

Apr 21
Apr 22

Moving to a New Pasture

The LORD is my shepherd;
I shall not want.
— Psalm 23:1

Your notes on **Psalm 23:1-3** and **John 10:11-18**:

Your answers to the devotional questions on April 22:

Your prayers:

Apr 23

Apr 24

Rod and Staff

Even though I walk through the valley of the shadow of death, I will fear no evil, for you are with me; your rod and your staff, they comfort me.
– *Psalm 23:4*

Your notes on **Psalm 23:1-4** and **1 Samuel 17:32-37**:

Your answers to the devotional questions on April 24:

Your prayers:

Apr 25

Apr 26

The Pursuit of Sinners

Surely goodness and mercy shall follow me all the days of my life, and I shall dwell in the house of the LORD forever.
– *Psalm 23:6*

Your notes on **Psalm 23:5-6** and **Luke 15:1-7**:

Your answers to the devotional questions on April 26:

Your prayers:

The LORD of Hosts

Lift up your heads, O gates! And lift them up, O ancient doors, that the King of glory may come in. Who is this King of glory? The LORD of hosts, he is the King of glory!
– *Psalm 24:9-10*

Your notes on **Psalm 24:1-10**:

Your answers to the devotional questions on April 28:

Your prayers:

Apr 29

Apr 30

Fearless Stephen

The LORD is my light and my salvation; whom shall I fear?
– *Psalm 27:1a*

Your notes on **Psalm 27:1-5** and **Acts 7:54-60**:

Your answers to the devotional questions on April 30:

Your prayers:

May 1

May 2

A Gentle Reminder

Wait for the LORD; be strong,
and let your heart take
courage; wait for the LORD!
– Psalm 27:14

Your notes on **Psalm 27:7-14** and **Romans 5:3-5**:

Your answers to the devotional questions on May 2:

Your prayers:

May
3

May
4

Offering Reassurance

The LORD is my strength and
my shield; in him my heart
trusts, and I am helped.
– *Psalm 28:7a*

Your notes on **Psalm 28:1-2, 6-9** and **1 Samuel 1:12-18**:

Your answers to the devotional questions on May 4:

Your prayers:

A Pre-Fight Blessing

The LORD gives strength to
his people; the LORD blesses
his people with peace.
– *Psalm 29:11 (NIV)*

Your notes on **Psalm 29:1-11**:

Your answers to the devotional questions on May 6:

Your prayers:

May 7

May 8

Plenty and Famine

Oh, how abundant is your goodness, which you have stored up for those who fear you and worked for those who take refuge in you, in the sight of the children of mankind!
– *Psalm 31:19*

Your notes on **Psalm 31:1-5, 9-10, 19-24**:

Your answers to the devotional questions on May 8:

Your prayers:

Wee Little Man in Jericho

I acknowledged my sin to you, and I did not cover my iniquity; I said, "I will confess my transgressions to the LORD," and you forgave the iniquity of my sin.
– *Psalm 32:5*

Your notes on **Psalm 32:1-5** and **Luke 19:1-10**:

Your answers to the devotional questions on May 10:

Your prayers:

May 11

May 12

Great and Good

I sought the LORD, and he answered me and delivered me from all my fears.
– Psalm 34:4

Your notes on **Psalm 34:1-7, 15-22**:

Your answers to the devotional questions on May 12:

Your prayers:

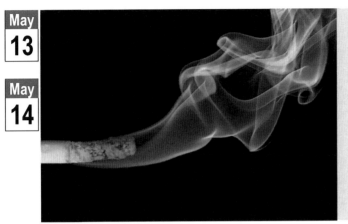

| May 13 | |
| May 14 | |

"Person to Person"

Those who look to him are radiant, and their faces shall never be ashamed.
– *Psalm 34:5*

Your notes on **Psalm 34:1-7** and **2 Corinthians 3:12-18**:

Your answers to the devotional questions on May 14:

Your prayers:

May 15

May 16

Taste and See

Oh, taste and see that the LORD is good! Blessed is the man who takes refuge in him!
– *Psalm 34:8*

Your notes on **Psalm 34:8-14** and **John 2:6-11**:

Your answers to the devotional questions on May 16:

Your prayers:

You Are Opposed

Many are the afflictions of the righteous, but the LORD delivers him out of them all.
— *Psalm 34:19*

Your notes on **Psalm 34:15-22** and **1 Peter 5:6-11**:

Your answers to the devotional questions on May 18:

Your prayers:

May 19

May 20

The Desires of Your Heart

Delight yourself in the LORD,
and he will give you the
desires of your heart.
– *Psalm 37:4*

Your notes on **Psalm 37:3-7, 16-19**:

Your answers to the devotional questions on May 20:

Your prayers:

May 21

May 22

Stand Up Eight

The steps of a man are established by the LORD, when he delights in his way; though he fall, he shall not be cast headlong, for the LORD upholds his hand.
– *Psalm 37:23-24*

Your notes on **Psalm 37:23-31, 39-40**:

Your answers to the devotional questions on May 22:

Your prayers:

May 23

May 24

The Patience of Joseph

I waited patiently for the LORD; he inclined to me and heard my cry. He drew me up from the pit of destruction, out of the miry bog, and set my feet upon a rock, making my steps secure.
– Psalm 40:1-2

Your notes on **Psalm 40:1-4** and **Genesis 50:15-21**:

Your answers to the devotional questions on May 24:

Your prayers:

May 25

May 26

A Mighty Fortress

God is our refuge and
strength, a very present
help in trouble.
– *Psalm 46:1*

Your notes on **Psalm 46:1-11**:

Your answers to the devotional questions on May 26:

Your prayers:

May 27

May 28

It Is Well

Cast your cares on the LORD
and he will sustain you; he
will never let the righteous
be shaken.
-- *Psalm 55:22 (NIV)*

Your notes on **Psalm 55:1-5, 16-22**:

Your answers to the devotional questions on May 28:

Your prayers:

May 29

May 30

IN GOD WE TRUST

When I am afraid, I put my trust in you. In God, whose word I praise, in God I trust; I shall not be afraid.
– Psalm 56:3-4a

Your notes on **Psalm 56:1-4, 8-11** and **Mark 9:17-18a, 21-24**:

Your answers to the devotional questions on May 30:

Your prayers:

May
31

Jun
1

The Best Things in Life

Because your steadfast love
is better than life,
my lips will praise you.
– Psalm 63:3

Your notes on **Psalm 63:1-11**:

Your answers to the devotional questions on June 1:

Your prayers:

Jun
2

Jun
3

(Good) News Flash!

The Lord gives the word;
the women who announce
the news are a great host.
— *Psalm 68:11*

Your notes on **Psalm 68:7-13** and **Luke 24:1-10**:

Your answers to the devotional questions on June 3:

Your prayers:

Doubting Disciples

You ascended on high,
leading a host of captives
in your train.
– Psalm 68:18a

Your notes on **Psalm 68:15-20** and **Acts 2:1-4, 14, 36**:

Your answers to the devotional questions on June 5:

Your prayers:

Jun
6

Jun
7

You Can Depend on Me

Be to me a rock of refuge,
to which I may continually
come; you have given the
command to save me, for
you are my rock
and my fortress.
– Psalm 71:3

Your notes on **Psalm 71:1-12**:

Your answers to the devotional questions on June 7:

Your prayers:

A Rock Becomes a Failure

My flesh and my heart may
fail, but God is the strength
of my heart and
my portion forever.
— *Psalm 73:26*

Your notes on **Psalm 73:1-5, 21-28**:

Your answers to the devotional questions on June 9:

Your prayers:

Jun 10

Jun 11

A German Requiem

How lovely is your dwelling place, O LORD of hosts!
— *Psalm 84:1*

Your notes on **Psalm 84:1-7** and **John 14:1-6**:

Your answers to the devotional questions on June 11:

Your prayers:

Groundhog Day

For a day in your courts
is better than
a thousand elsewhere.
– Psalm 84:10a

Your notes on **Psalm 84:1-13**:

Your answers to the devotional questions on June 13:

Your prayers:

Jun 14

Jun 15

Forgiving Every Penny

For you, O Lord, are good
and forgiving, abounding
in steadfast love to all
who call upon you.
– *Psalm 86:5*

Your notes on **Psalm 86:1-10** and **Matthew 18:15-17**:

Your answers to the devotional questions on June 15:

Your prayers:

Jun **16**

Jun **17**

Marvelous Things

Oh sing to the LORD a new song, for he has done marvelous things! His right hand and his holy arm have worked salvation for him.
— *Psalm 98:1*

Your notes on **Psalm 98:1-9** and **Job 5:8-11**:

Your answers to the devotional questions on June 17:

Your prayers:

Jun 18

Jun 19

A Joyful Noise

Make a joyful noise to
the LORD, all the earth!
— *Psalm 100:1*

Your notes on **Psalm 100** and **Psalm 150**:

Your answers to the devotional questions on June 19:

Your prayers:

Jun 20

 Jun 21

Forever

For the Lord is good; his steadfast love endures forever, and his faithfulness to all generations.
– Psalm 100:5

Your notes on **Psalm 100** and **Psalm 136:1-7**:

Your answers to the devotional questions on June 21:

Your prayers:

Field of Peace

Bless the LORD, O my soul,
and forget not all his benefits,
who forgives all your iniquity,
who heals all your diseases.
– *Psalm 103:2–3*

Your notes on **Psalm 103:1-5** and **Psalm 51:1-2, 7-12**:

Your answers to the devotional questions on June 23:

Your prayers:

Jun 24

Jun 25

Schindler's Pit

[The Lord] redeems your life
from the pit [and] crowns you
with steadfast love and mercy.
-- *Psalm 103:4*

Your notes on **Psalm 103:1-5** and **Psalm 40:1-5**:

Your answers to the devotional questions on June 25:

Your prayers:

Jun 26

Jun 27

A Spiritual Diet

[The Lord] satisfies you with good so that your youth is renewed like the eagle's.
-- *Psalm 103:5*

Your notes on **Psalm 103:1-5** and **Isaiah 40:28-31**:

Your answers to the devotional questions on June 27:

Your prayers:

Jun 28

Jun 29

Fighting for Justice

The LORD works
righteousness and justice
for all who are oppressed.
– *Psalm 103:6*

Your notes on **Psalm 103:6-14** and **Micah 6:6-8**:

Your answers to the devotional questions on June 29:

Your prayers:

Jun 30

Jul 1

To Infinity, and Beyond

As far as the east is from the west, so far does he remove our transgressions from us.
– *Psalm 103:12*

Your notes on **Psalm 103:6-14** and **Ephesians 3:14-19**:

Your answers to the devotional questions on July 1:

Your prayers:

Jul 2

Jul 3

Running Away Naked

Who can proclaim the mighty acts of the LORD or fully declare his praise?
— *Psalm 106:2*

Your notes on **Psalm 106:1-8** and **2 Timothy 4:9-11**:

Your answers to the devotional questions on July 3:

Your prayers:

Jul
4

Jul
5

Introverts Unite!

With my mouth I will give great thanks to the LORD; I will praise him in the midst of the throng. For he stands at the right hand of the needy one, to save him from those who condemn his soul to death.
– Psalm 109:30-31

Your notes on **Psalm 109:1-5, 26-31**:

Your answers to the devotional questions on July 5:

Your prayers:

Jul 6

Jul 7

Drinking Like Dogs

The LORD is on my side;
I will not fear. What can
man do to me?
– *Psalm 118:6*

Your notes on **Psalm 118:1-9** and **Psalm 124:1-8**:

Your answers to the devotional questions on July 7:

Your prayers:

Jul 8

Jul 9

Salvation on a Mountain

The LORD is my strength
and my song; he has
become my salvation.
– *Psalm 118:14*

Your notes on **Psalm 118:14-24** and **Genesis 22:6-8**:

Your answers to the devotional questions on July 9:

Your prayers:

Jul 10

Jul 11

Redemption in Hickory

It is good for me that I
was afflicted, that I might
learn your statutes.
– Psalm 119:71

Your notes on **Psalm 119:65-74** and **2 Corinthians 4:16-18**:

Your answers to the devotional questions on July 11:

Your prayers:

Jul 12

 Jul 13

Sword of the Spirit

Your word is a lamp to my
feet and a light to my path.
– Psalm 119:105

Your notes on **Psalm 119:103-112** and **Hebrews 4:9-12**:

Your answers to the devotional questions on July 13:

Your prayers:

Jul 14

Jul 15

The Bible's Knuckleheads

You are my hiding place and my shield; I hope in your word.
– *Psalm 119:114*

Your notes on **Psalm 119:108-117** and **Romans 5:1-5**:

Your answers to the devotional questions on July 15:

Your prayers:

Good News for the Simple

The unfolding of your words
gives light; it imparts
understanding to the simple.
-- *Psalm 119:130*

Your notes on **Psalm 119:125-135** and **1 Corinthians 1:20-25**:

Your answers to the devotional questions on July 17:

Your prayers:

Smelling the Color Nine

In my distress I called to the
LORD, and he answered me.
-- Psalm 120:1

Your notes on **Psalm 120:1-4** and **1 Kings 19:11-13**:

Your answers to the devotional questions on July 19:

Your prayers:

Jul
20

Jul
21

Special Agent

My help comes from
the LORD, who made
heaven and earth.
-- *Psalm 121:2*

Your notes on **Psalm 121** and **Hebrews 1:1-4**:

Your answers to the devotional questions on July 21:

Your prayers:

Jul 22

Jul 23

A Wonderful Life

The LORD has done great things for us, and we are filled with joy.
-- *Psalm 126:3 (NIV)*

Your notes on **Psalm 126** and **Psalm 71:17-21**:

Your answers to the devotional questions on July 23:

Your prayers:

Jul 24

Jul 25

Steadfast and Plentiful

O Israel, hope in the LORD!
For with the LORD there is
steadfast love, and with him
is plentiful redemption.
-- Psalm 130:7

Your notes on **Psalm 130** and **Psalm 36:5-9**:

Your answers to the devotional questions on July 25:

Your prayers:

Jul 26

Jul 27

Knitted Together

For you formed my inward parts; you knitted me together in my mother's womb. I praise you, for I am fearfully and wonderfully made.
-- *Psalm 139:13-14a*

Your notes on **Psalm 139:7-18**:

Your answers to the devotional questions on July 27:

Your prayers:

| Jul 28 |
| Jul 29 |

Lift Up Your Voice in Praise

Praise the LORD! For it is good
to sing praises to our God;
for it is pleasant, and a song
of praise is fitting.
-- Psalm 147:1

Your notes on **Psalm 147:1-6** and **Psalm 148:1-6**:

Your answers to the devotional questions on July 29:

Your prayers:

Jul 30

Jul 31

A City Under Siege

He heals the brokenhearted
and binds up their wounds.
-- *Psalm 147:3*

Your notes on **Psalm 147:1-6** and **Psalm 34:15-18**:

Your answers to the devotional questions on July 31:

Your prayers:

Bigger Than the Boogie Man

Great is our Lord, and abundant
in power; his understanding
is beyond measure.
-- *Psalm 147:5*

Your notes on **Psalm 147:1-6** and **Romans 11:33-36**:

Your answers to the devotional questions on August 2:

Your prayers:

Aug 3

Aug 4

Lord, Have Mercy

The LORD lifts up the humble; he casts the wicked to the ground.
-- *Psalm 147:6*

Your notes on **Psalm 147:1-6** and **Ephesians 2:1-9**:

Your answers to the devotional questions on August 4:

Your prayers:

Aug 5

 Aug 6

Unbroken in Christ

His delight is not in the strength of the horse, nor his pleasure in the legs of a man, but the LORD takes pleasure in those who fear him, in those who hope in his steadfast love.
-- *Psalm 147:10-11*

Your notes on **Psalm 147:7-18**:

Your answers to the devotional questions on August 6:

Your prayers:

Aug 7

Aug 8

A Dazzling Adornment

For the LORD takes pleasure in his people; he adorns the humble with salvation.
-- *Psalm 149:4*

Your notes on **Psalm 149** and **1 Peter 3:14-16**:

Your answers to the devotional questions on August 8:

Your prayers:

Aug 9

Aug 10

Risking the Den

But whoever listens to me will dwell secure and will be at ease, without dread of disaster.
-- *Proverbs 1:33*

Your notes on **Proverbs 1:29-33** and **Daniel 6:16-22**:

Your answers to the devotional questions on August 10:

Your prayers:

Aug 11

Aug 12

The Value of Wisdom

For the LORD gives
wisdom; from his mouth
come knowledge
and understanding.
-- *Proverbs 2:6*

Your notes on **Proverbs 2:1-15**:

Your answers to the devotional questions on August 12:

Your prayers:

Aug 13

Aug 14

Peace on the Battlefield

My son, do not forget my teaching, but let your heart keep my commandments, for length of days and years of life and peace they will add to you.
-- Proverbs 3:1-2

Your notes on **Proverbs 3:1-4** and **Mark 12:28-34**:

Your answers to the devotional questions on August 14:

Your prayers:

Aug 15

Aug 16

The Trust of Ananias

Trust in the LORD with all your heart, and do not lean on your own understanding. In all your ways acknowledge him, and he will make straight your paths.
-- *Proverbs 3:5-6*

Your notes on **Proverbs 3:5-8** and **Philemon 17-22**:

Your answers to the devotional questions on August 16:

Your prayers:

Aug 17

Aug 18

Still Standing after 15

My son, do not despise
the LORD's discipline or
be weary of his reproof,
for the LORD reproves him
whom he loves, as a father
the son in whom he delights.
-- *Proverbs 3:11-12*

Your notes on **Proverbs 3:9-12** and **Hebrews 12:7-11**:

Your answers to the devotional questions on August 18:

Your prayers:

Aug 19

Aug 20

The Wisdom of Hazel

Blessed is the one who finds wisdom, and the one who gets understanding, for the gain from her is better than gain from silver and her profit better than gold.
-- *Proverbs 3:13-14*

Your notes on **Proverbs 3:13-27**:

Your answers to the devotional questions on August 20:

Your prayers:

Aug 21

Aug 22

Shading Our Eyes

But the path of the righteous is like the light of dawn, which shines brighter and brighter until full day.
-- *Proverbs 4:18*

Your notes on **Proverbs 4:10-23**:

Your answers to the devotional questions on August 22:

Your prayers:

Aug 23

Aug 24

Surprise!

For a man's ways are before the eyes of the LORD, and he ponders all his paths.
– *Proverbs 5:21*

Your notes on **Proverbs 5:1-4, 20-23** and **Psalm 16:7-11**:

Your answers to the devotional questions on August 24:

Your prayers:

Aug 25

Aug 26

A Straight-A Student

The fear of the LORD is the beginning of wisdom, and the knowledge of the Holy One is insight.
– Proverbs 9:10

Your notes on **Proverbs 9:7-12** and **James 1:22-25**:

Your answers to the devotional questions on August 26:

Your prayers:

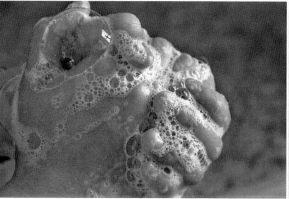

Aug 27

Aug 28

Keeping Your Hands Clean

The wicked earns deceptive wages, but one who sows righteousness gets a sure reward.
– *Proverbs 11:18*

Your notes on **Proverbs 11:10-22**:

Your answers to the devotional questions on August 28:

Your prayers:

Aug 29

Aug 30

A Good Neighbor

A generous person will prosper; whoever refreshes others will be refreshed.
– *Proverbs 11:25 (NIV)*

Your notes on **Proverbs 11:23-30** and **John 4:39-42**:

Your answers to the devotional questions on August 30:

Your prayers:

Aug 31

Sep 1

Rotting Bones

A heart at peace gives life to the body, but envy rots the bones.
– *Proverbs 14:30 (NIV)*

Your notes on **Proverbs 14:26-35** and **James 4:10-12**:

Your answers to the devotional questions on September 1:

Your prayers:

Sep 2

Sep 3

My Dog's Better

Whoever oppresses a poor man insults his Maker, but he who is generous to the needy honors him.
– Proverbs 14:31

Your notes on **Proverbs 14:26-35** and **Philippians 2:3-4**:

Your answers to the devotional questions on September 3:

Your prayers:

Sep 4

Sep 5

The First Evangelist

Commit your work to the
Lord, and your plans
will be established.
– Proverbs 16:3

Your notes on **Proverbs 16:1-9** and **Acts 8:35-40**:

Your answers to the devotional questions on September 5:

Your prayers:

Sep
6

Sep
7

What's in a Name?

The name of the LORD is a strong tower; the righteous man runs into it and is safe.
– Proverbs 18:10

Your notes on **Proverbs 18:8-16** and **Philippians 2:9-11**:

Your answers to the devotional questions on September 7:

Your prayers:

Sep 8

Sep 9

Sharpen His Saw

Iron sharpens iron, and one
man sharpens another.
– *Proverbs 27:17*

Your notes on **Proverbs 27:17-19** and **1 Corinthians 12:12-13a, 21-27**:

Your answers to the devotional questions on September 9:

Your prayers:

Sep 10

Sep 11

Turn, Turn, Turn

For everything there is
a season, and a time for
every matter under heaven.
– *Ecclesiastes 3:1*

Your notes on **Ecclesiastes 3:1-8**:

Your answers to the devotional questions on September 11:

Your prayers:

Beauty at the Well

He has made everything
beauty in its time.
– Ecclesiastes 3:11a

Your notes on **Ecclesiastes 3:9-13** and **John 4:19-26**:

Your answers to the devotional questions on September 13:

Your prayers:

Sep 14

Sep 15

Songs or Tales

Two are better than one, because they have a good reward for their toil. For if they fall, one will lift up his fellow.
– *Ecclesiastes 4:9-10a*

Your notes on **Ecclesiastes 4:9-12** and **Mark 6:7-13**:

Your answers to the devotional questions on September 15:

Your prayers:

Sep 16

Sep 17

A Tenacious Center

And though a man might prevail against one who is alone, two will withstand him—a threefold cord is not quickly broken.
— *Ecclesiastes 4:12*

Your notes on **Ecclesiastes 4:9-12** and **Galatians 2:17-21**:

Your answers to the devotional questions on September 17:

Your prayers:

Sep 18

Sep 19

An Unspectacular Life

Now all has been heard; here is the conclusion of the matter: Fear God and keep his commandments, for this is the duty of man.
– Ecclesiastes 12:13

Your notes on **Ecclesiastes 12:9-14** and **Ecclesiastes 1:12-15**:

Your answers to the devotional questions on September 19:

Your prayers:

The Power That Heals

Set me as a seal
upon your heart.
– *Song of Solomon 8:6a*

Your notes on **Song of Solomon 8:4-7** and **2 Corinthians 1:20-22**:

Your answers to the devotional questions on September 21:

Your prayers:

Sep 22

Sep 23

700 Years in the Making

Therefore the Lord himself will give you a sign. Behold, the virgin shall conceive and bear a son, and shall call his name Immanuel.
– Isaiah 7:14

Your notes on **Isaiah 7:10-16** and **Matthew 1:20-25**:

Your answers to the devotional questions on September 23:

Your prayers:

Lighting the Darkness

The people who walked in darkness have seen a great light; those who dwelt in a land of deep darkness, on them has light shone.
– *Isaiah 9:2*

Your notes on **Isaiah 9:1-5** and **John 8:12**:

Your answers to the devotional questions on September 25:

Your prayers:

At the Back of the Stage

For to us a child is born, to us a son is given; and the government shall be upon his shoulder, and his name shall be called Wonderful Counselor, Mighty God, Everlasting Father, Prince of Peace.
– *Isaiah 9:6*

Your notes on **Isaiah 9:1-7**:

Your answers to the devotional questions on September 27:

Your prayers:

Sep 28

Sep 29

Just Off Red Square

Behold, God is my salvation;
I will trust, and will not be
afraid; for the LORD God is
my strength and my song,
and he has become
my salvation.
– Isaiah 12:2

Your notes on **Isaiah 12:1-6** and **Isaiah 25:8-9**:

Your answers to the devotional questions on September 29:

Your prayers:

Sep 30

Oct 1

The Wild Man

O LORD, you are my God;
I will exalt you; I will praise
your name, for you have
done wonderful things,
plans formed of old,
faithful and sure.
– Isaiah 25:1

Your notes on **Isaiah 25:1-5** and **Joel 2:26-27**:

Your answers to the devotional questions on October 1:

Your prayers:

The Rolling Thunder

For you have been a stronghold to the poor, a stronghold to the needy in his distress, a shelter from the storm and a shade from the heat.
– Isaiah 25:4a

Your notes on **Isaiah 25:1-5** and **Psalm 91:1-6**:

Your answers to the devotional questions on October 3:

Your prayers:

Oct 4

Oct 5

Perfect Peace for "Pistol"

You keep him in perfect peace whose mind is stayed on you, because he trusts in you.
– Isaiah 26:3

Your notes on **Isaiah 26:1-6** and **John 14:25-27**:

Your answers to the devotional questions on October 5:

Your prayers:

Oct 6

Oct 7

The Rock of Ages

Trust in the LORD forever,
for the LORD GOD is an
everlasting rock.
– *Isaiah 26:4*

Your notes on **Isaiah 26:1-6, Habakkuk 1:12,** and **Acts 4:10-12**:

Your answers to the devotional questions on October 7:

Your prayers:

Oct 8

Oct 9

Waiting for God

Therefore the LORD waits to be gracious to you, and therefore he exalts himself to show mercy to you. For the LORD is a God of justice; blessed are all those who wait for him.
— *Isaiah 30:18*

Your notes on **Isaiah 30:15-22**:

Your answers to the devotional questions on October 9:

Your prayers:

Oct 10

Oct 11

The Crooked Straight

Every valley shall be lifted up, and every mountain and hill be made low; the uneven ground shall become level, and the rough places a plain.
– Isaiah 40:4

Your notes on **Isaiah 40:1-11**:

Your answers to the devotional questions on October 11:

Your prayers:

Oct 12

Oct 13

The Forgotten Part

And the glory of the LORD shall be revealed, and all flesh shall see it together, for the mouth of the LORD has spoken.
– Isaiah 40:5

Your notes on **Isaiah 40:1-11**:

Your answers to the devotional questions on October 13:

Your prayers:

Oct 14

Oct 15

Extra! Extra!

Have you not known? Have you not heard? The LORD is the everlasting God, the Creator of the ends of the earth. He does not faint or grow weary; his understanding is unsearchable.
– Isaiah 40:28

Your notes on **Isaiah 40:21-28**:

Your answers to the devotional questions on October 15:

Your prayers:

Oct 16

Oct 17

The Value of Strength

He gives power to the faint,
and to him who has no might
he increases strength.
– Isaiah 40:29

Your notes on **Isaiah 40:27-31** and **2 Corinthians 12:7-10**:

Your answers to the devotional questions on October 17:

Your prayers:

Oct 18

Oct 19

No More Weariness

Even youths grow tired and weary, and young men stumble and fall; but those who hope in the LORD will renew their strength. They will soar on wings like eagles; they will run and not grow weary, they will walk and not be faint.
— *Isaiah 40:30-31 (NIV)*

Your notes on **Isaiah 40:27-31** and **Matthew 11:25-30**:

Your answers to the devotional questions on October 19:

Your prayers:

Oct 20

Oct 21

A Firm Foundation

Fear not, for I am with you; be not dismayed, for I am your God; I will strengthen you, I will help you, I will uphold you with my righteous right hand.
— *Isaiah 41:10*

Your notes on **Isaiah 41:1-10**:

Your answers to the devotional questions on October 21:

Your prayers:

Oct
22

Oct
23

450 vs. 1

For I, the LORD your God,
hold your right hand; it is I
who say to you, "Fear not, I
am the one who helps you."
— *Isaiah 41:13*

Your notes on **Isaiah 41:11-13** and **Isaiah 43:1-7**:

Your answers to the devotional questions on October 23:

Your prayers:

A Nu Thang

Behold, I am doing a
new thing; now it springs
forth, do you not perceive it?
I will make a way
in the wilderness and
rivers in the desert.
– *Isaiah 43:19*

Your notes on **Isaiah 43:16-25**:

Your answers to the devotional questions on October 25:

Your prayers:

Oct 26

Oct 27

Overblown?

I will go before you and level
the exalted places, I will
break in pieces the doors
of bronze and cut through
the bars of iron.
— *Isaiah 45:2*

Your notes on **Isaiah 45:1-8**:

Your answers to the devotional questions on October 27:

Your prayers:

Like a Flint

But the LORD GOD helps me;
therefore I have not been
disgraced; therefore I have
set my face like a flint,
and I know that I shall not
be put to shame.
– *Isaiah 50:7*

Your notes on **Isaiah 50:4-11**:

Your answers to the devotional questions on October 28:

Your prayers:

Oct 30

Oct 31

Falsely Accused

He was despised and rejected by men, a man of sorrows and acquainted with grief; and as one from whom men hide their faces he was despised, and we esteemed him not.
– Isaiah 53:3

Your notes on **Isaiah 53:1-6** and **Psalm 118:19-23**:

Your answers to the devotional questions on October 30:

Your prayers:

Nov 1

Nov 2

Not a Beast

Surely he has borne
our griefs and carried
our sorrows; yet we
esteemed him stricken,
smitten by God, and afflicted.
– *Isaiah 53:4*

Your notes on **Isaiah 53:1-6** and **Philippians 2:5-8**:

Your answers to the devotional questions on November 2:

Your prayers:

Nov 3

Nov 4

Amazing Love!

But he was pierced for our transgressions; he was crushed for our iniquities; upon him was the chastisement that brought us peace, and with his wounds we are healed.
– Isaiah 53:5

Your notes on **Isaiah 53:4-11**:

Your answers to the devotional questions on November 4:

Your prayers:

Nov 5

Nov 6

Paul the Sheep

All we like sheep have gone astray; we have turned— every one—to his own way; and the LORD has laid on him the iniquity of us all.
— *Isaiah 53:6*

Your notes on **Isaiah 53:3-6** and **1 Peter 2:21b-25**:

Your answers to the devotional questions on November 6:

Your prayers:

Nov 7

Nov 8

No Separation

No weapon that is fashioned against you shall succeed, and you shall refute every tongue that rises against you in judgment.
– Isaiah 54:17a

Your notes on **Isaiah 54:11-17**:

Your answers to the devotional questions on November 8:

Your prayers:

Nov 9

Nov 10

Are You the One?

The Spirit of the LORD GOD is upon me, because the LORD has anointed me to bring good news to the poor; he has sent me to bind up the brokenhearted, to proclaim liberty to the captives, and the opening of the prison to those who are bound.
– Isaiah 61:1

Your notes on **Isaiah 61:1-3** and **Luke 4:16-21**:

Your answers to the devotional questions on November 10:

Your prayers:

Nov 11

Nov 12

Feeling God's Pleasure

Before I formed you in the
womb I knew you.
— *Jeremiah 1:5a*

Your notes on **Jeremiah 1:1-10**:

Your answers to the devotional questions on November 12:

Your prayers:

Nov 13

Nov 14

Back in Kindergarten

But the LORD said to me, "Do not say, 'I am only a youth'; for to all to whom I send you, you shall go, and whatever I command you, you shall speak."
– *Jeremiah 1:7*

Your notes on **Jeremiah 1:6-10** and **1 Timothy 4:11-16**:

Your answers to the devotional questions on November 14:

Your prayers:

Nov 15

Nov 16

Healing in the Dark

Heal me, O LORD, and I
shall be healed; save me,
and I shall be saved,
for you are my praise.
– *Jeremiah 17:14*

Your notes on **Jeremiah 17:7-8, 12-18**:

Your answers to the devotional questions on November 16:

Your prayers:

The Good Old Days

Behold, the days are coming, declares the LORD, when I will raise up for David a righteous Branch, and he shall reign as king and deal wisely, and shall execute justice and righteousness in the land.
– *Jeremiah 23:5*

Your notes on **Jeremiah 23:1-8**:

Your answers to the devotional questions on November 18:

Your prayers:

The Master Planner

"For I know the plans I have for you," declares the Lord, "plans to prosper you and not to harm you, plans to give you hope and a future."
– *Jeremiah 29:11 (NIV)*

Your notes on **Jeremiah 29:1, 4-13**:

Your answers to the devotional questions on November 20:

Your prayers:

Nov 21

Nov 22

The One Thing
Call to me and I will answer
you, and will tell you great
and hidden things that
you have not known.
– *Jeremiah 33:3*

Your notes on **Jeremiah 33:1-9**:

Your answers to the devotional questions on November 22:

Your prayers:

Nov 23

Nov 24

The Gift of Today

The steadfast love of the LORD never ceases; his mercies never come to an end; they are new every morning; great is your faithfulness.
– *Lamentations 3:22–23*

Your notes on **Lamentations 3:19-27** and **Psalm 30:1-5**:

Your answers to the devotional questions on November 24:

Your prayers:

Nov 25

Nov 26

Perseverance

The LORD is good to those
who wait for him, to the soul
who seeks him.
– *Lamentations 3:25*

Your notes on **Lamentations 3:19-27** and **Psalm 27:11-14**:

Your answers to the devotional questions on November 26:

Your prayers:

Minute by Minute

But you, O LORD, reign
forever; your throne endures
to all generations.
– *Lamentations 5:19*

Your notes on **Lamentations 5:14-21** and **Revelation 4:8-11**:

Your answers to the devotional questions on November 28:

Your prayers:

Your True Name

And I will give you a new heart, and a new spirit I will put within you. And I will remove the heart of stone from your flesh and give you a heart of flesh.
– *Ezekiel 36:26*

Your notes on **Ezekiel 36:22-30**:

Your answers to the devotional questions on November 30:

Your prayers:

From a Birmingham Jail

If this be so, our God whom we serve is able to deliver us from the burning fiery furnace, and he will deliver us out of your hand, O king. But if not, be it known to you, O king, that we will not serve your gods or worship the golden image that you have set up.
— *Daniel 3:17-18*

Your notes on **Daniel 3:14-18, 23-25**:

Your answers to the devotional questions on December 2:

Your prayers:

Dec 3

Dec 4

New and Improved

His dominion is an everlasting dominion, which shall not pass away, and his kingdom one that shall not be destroyed.
– Daniel 7:14b

Your notes on **Daniel 7:9-10, 13-14** and **Hebrews 13:5-8**:

Your answers to the devotional questions on December 4:

Your prayers:

Dec
5

Dec
6

Extravagant Grace

The Lord our God is merciful
and forgiving, even though we
have rebelled against him.
– Daniel 9:9 (NIV)

Your notes on **Daniel 9:4-10, 17-18**:

Your answers to the devotional questions on December 6:

Your prayers:

Dec 7

Dec 8

Fallow Ground

Break up your fallow ground,
for it is the time to seek the
LORD, that he may come and
rain righteousness upon you.
— *Hosea 10:12b*

Your notes on **Hosea 10:1-2, 9-14a**:

Your answers to the devotional questions on December 8:

Your prayers:

Dec
9

Dec
10

A Better Man

Return to the Lord your God,
for he is gracious and merciful,
slow to anger, and abounding
in steadfast love.
– Joel 2:13b

Your notes on **Joel 2:10-17**:

Your answers to the devotional questions on December 10:

Your prayers:

Dec 11

Dec 12

Trusting and Obeying

And it shall come to pass
that everyone who calls
on the name of the LORD
shall be saved.
– Joel 2:32a

Your notes on **Joel 2:23-32**:

Your answers to the devotional questions on December 12:

Your prayers:

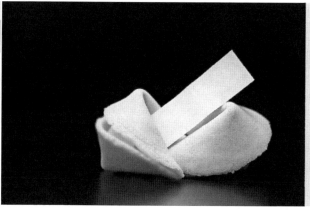

Good Fortune

For the LORD GOD does
nothing without revealing
his secret to his servants
the prophets.
– Amos 3:7

Your notes on **Amos 3:3-8** and **Matthew 13:10-15**:

Your answers to the devotional questions on December 14:

Your prayers:

Dec 15

Dec 16

Shameful Joy

But do not gloat over the day of your brother in the day of his misfortune.
– *Obadiah 12a*

Your notes on **Obadiah 12-15** and **Philippians 2:1-4**:

Your answers to the devotional questions on December 16:

Your prayers:

Dec 17

Dec 18

In the Belly

Then Jonah prayed to the LORD his God from the belly of the fish, saying, "I called out to the LORD, out of my distress, and he answered me; out of the belly of Sheol I cried, and you heard my voice."
– Jonah 2:1-2

Your notes on **Jonah 1:13–2:6**:

Your answers to the devotional questions on December 18:

Your prayers:

Dec 19

Dec 20

Crushing Your Sins

He will again have
compassion on us; he will
tread our iniquities underfoot.
You will cast all our sins into
the depths of the sea.
— *Micah 7:19*

Your notes on **Micah 7:18-20** and **Psalm 103:6-13**:

Your answers to the devotional questions on December 20:

Your prayers:

Dec 21

Dec 22

No More Mr. Nice Guy

The LORD is good,
a stronghold in
the day of trouble.
– *Nahum 1:7a*

Your notes on **Nahum 1:3-7** and **Matthew 23:1-5a, 27-28**:

Your answers to the devotional questions on December 22:

Your prayers:

Dec 23

Dec 24

Pay-It-Forward Joy

Yet I will rejoice in the LORD;
I will take joy in the God
of my salvation.
— *Habakkuk 3:18*

Your notes on **Habakkuk 3:1-6, 17-19**:

Your answers to the devotional questions on December 24:

Your prayers:

Dec 25

Dec 26

From a Distance

The LORD your God is
in your midst, a mighty one
who will save.
– *Zephaniah 3:17a*

Your notes on **Zephaniah 3:11-19**:

Your answers to the devotional questions on December 26:

Your prayers:

Your Glory Days

The latter glory of this house shall be greater than the former, says the LORD of hosts.
– *Haggai 2:9a*

Your notes on **Haggai 2:3-9**:

Your answers to the devotional questions on December 28:

Your prayers:

Shouting at Jesus

Rejoice greatly, O daughter
of Zion! Shout aloud, O
daughter of Jerusalem!
Behold, your king is coming
to you; righteous and
having salvation is he,
humble and mounted on
a donkey, on a colt,
the foal of a donkey.
– *Zechariah 9:9*

Your notes on **Zechariah 9:9-10, 14-17**:

Your answers to the devotional questions on December 30:

Your prayers:

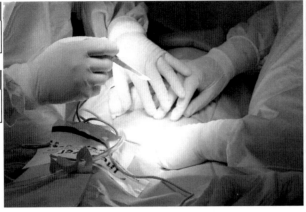

Whole Again

"But for you who fear my name, the sun of righteousness shall rise with healing in its wings."
– Malachi 4:2a

Your notes on **Malachi 4:1-6**:

Your answers to the devotional questions on January 1:

Your prayers: